e/E 1

Backyard Animals
Bats

Annalise Bekkering

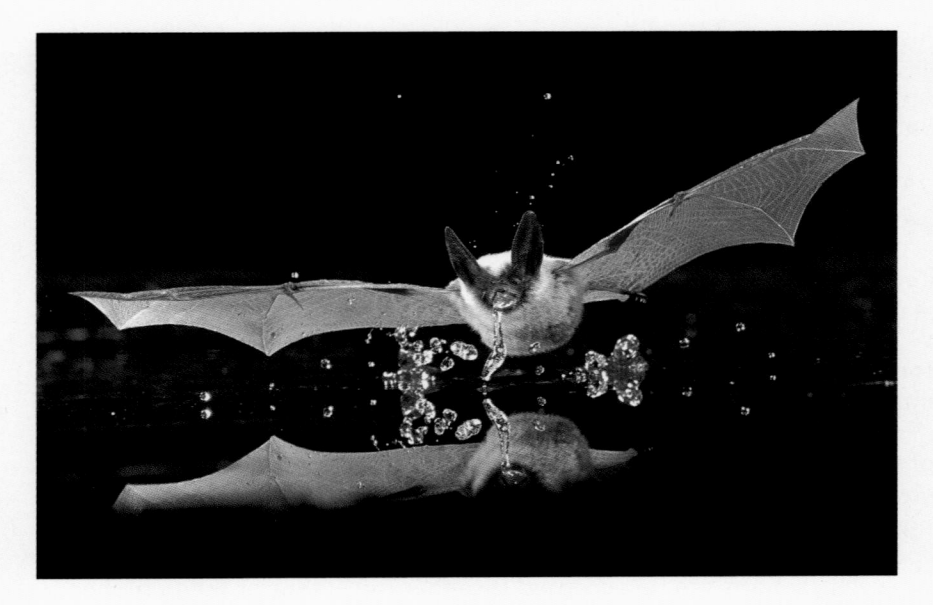

Weigl Publishers Inc.

Published by Weigl Publishers Inc.
350 5th Avenue, Suite 3304, PMB 6G
New York, NY 10118-0069
Website: www.weigl.com

Library of Congress Cataloging-in-Publication Data

Bekkering, Annalise.
 Bats / Annalise Bekkering.
    p. cm. -- (Backyard animals)
 Includes index.
 ISBN 978-1-60596-076-0 (hard cover : alk. paper) -- ISBN 978-1-60596-077-7 (soft
cover : alk. paper)
 1. Bats--Juvenile literature. I. Title.

 QL737.C5B389 2010
 599.4--dc22

                                      2008052056

Printed in China
1 2 3 4 5 6 7 8 9 0 13 12 11 10 09

Editor Heather C. Hudak
Design Terry Paulhus

Photo Credits

Every reasonable effort has been made to trace ownership and to obtain
permission to reprint copyright material. The publishers would be pleased
to have any errors or omissions brought to their attention so that they may
be corrected in subsequent printings.

Weigl acknowledges Getty Images as its primary image supplier for this title.

Aaron Jackson: Page 7, bottom right.

Contents

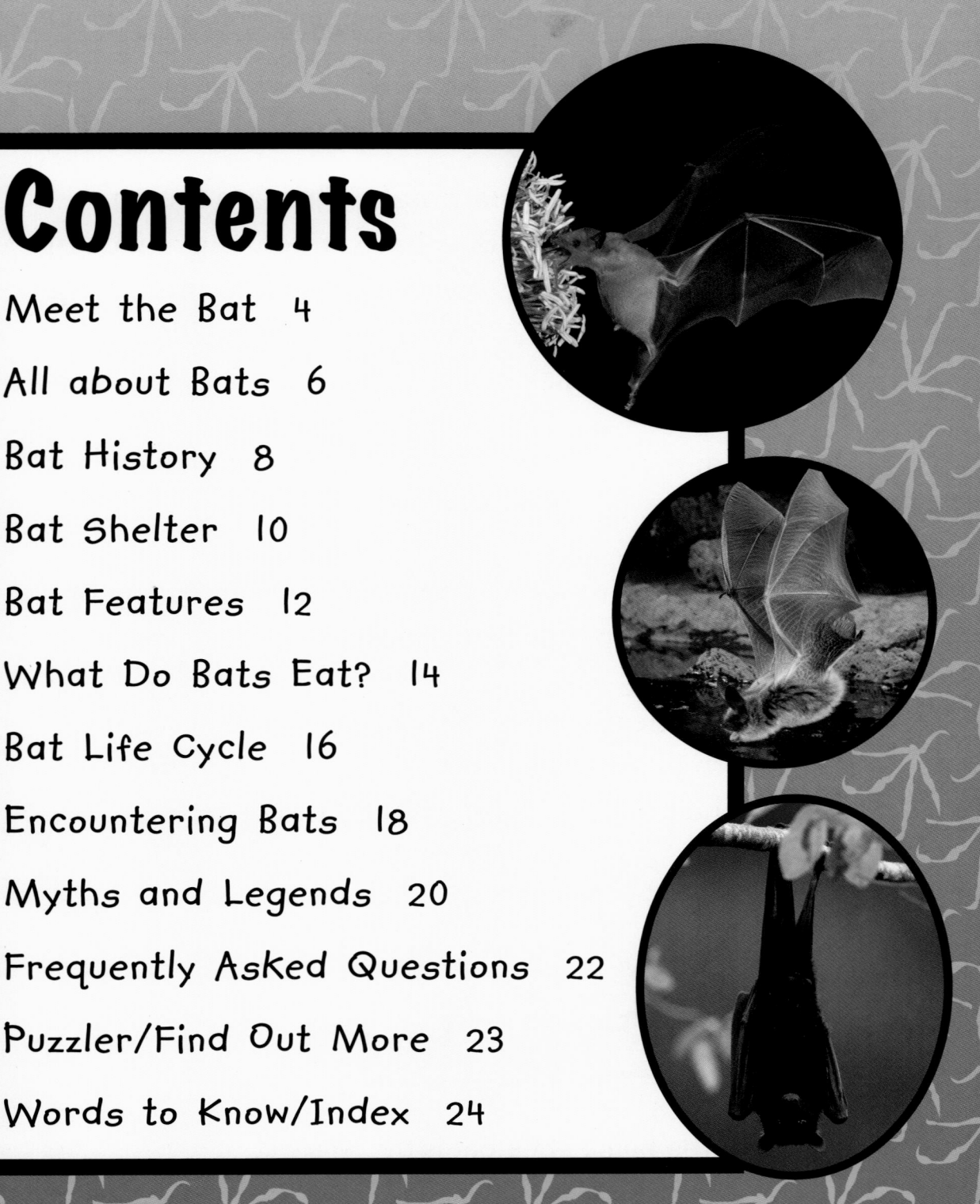

Meet the Bat

Bats are small, flying **mammals**. They are the only mammals that can fly. Bats have large wings made of two layers of skin. This skin stretches over their long finger bones and arms. It connects to the sides of the body and back legs.

Bats' bodies are covered in fur. They often have black or brown fur. It can also be gray, white, red, or orange.

Bats are clean animals. When they are not eating or sleeping, they spend time **grooming** themselves.

Bats live in nearly every part of the world, except for the North and South Poles. They eat mosquitos and bugs to help keep neighborhoods insect-free.

The bumblebee bat is the smallest bat in the world. It weighs less than a penny.

Some types of bats
can fly up to 60 miles
(97 kilometers) per hour.

All about Bats

There are almost 1,000 different **species** of bats throughout the world. Some bats are as big as large birds. Others are as small as mice. Bats can weigh between 0.07 ounces and 2.9 pounds (2 grams and 1.3 kilograms). The smallest bat in the world is only 1 inch (2.5 centimeters) long.

Bats are divided into two groups. Old World fruit bats live mostly in **tropical** areas, such as Africa, India, and Australia. These bats are also called megabats. Megabats mostly eat fruit and **nectar**. Microbats are smaller and live in many places around the world. Most microbats eat insects. Some also eat other small mammals and fish.

When bats feel threatened, they show their teeth and squeak loudly.

Where Bats Live

Vampire Bat

- Found in South and Central America

Little Brown Bat

- Found throughout North America

Indian Flying Fox Bat

- Found in India and other Asian countries

Mexican Free-tailed Bat

- Found in southern United States, Mexico, Chile, Argentina, southern Brazil, and the Greater and Lesser Antilles

Bat History

Bats have been on Earth for a very long time. The oldest bat **fossil** is about 50 million years old. The remains found in the fossil look much like bats today. This shows that the way bats look has changed very little over time.

Some people think bats are harmful animals. However, bats are helpful in many ways. Scientists have been able to make medicine from the **saliva** of vampire bats. This medicine is used to help people who have had heart attacks or **strokes.**

Bats produce droppings called guano. Guano is an excellent fertilizer for plants and crops.

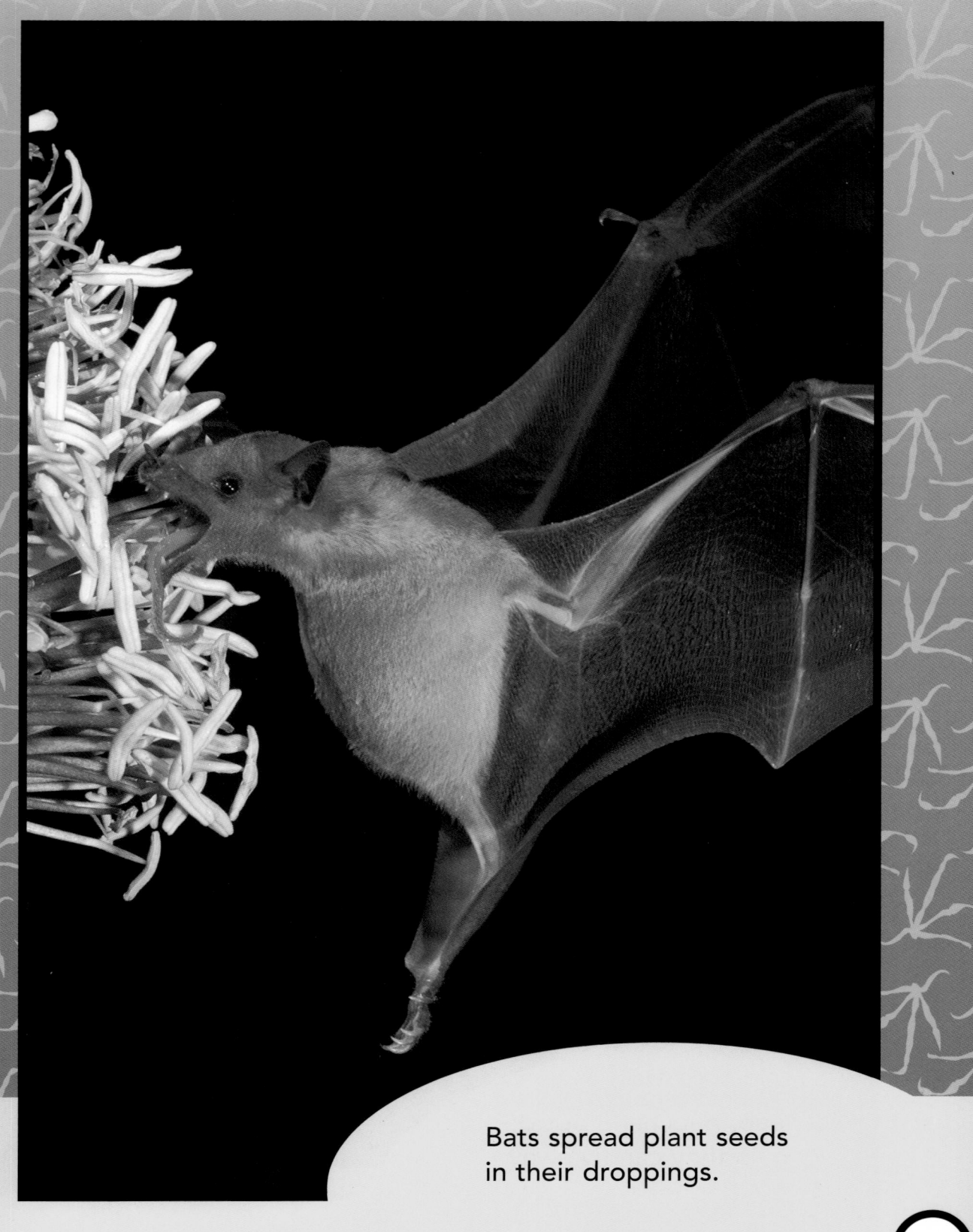

Bats spread plant seeds
in their droppings.

Bat Shelter

From tropical rain forests to the cold Arctic, bats live in most parts of the world. They can live in caves, holes in trees or rock walls, and buildings.

Many bats live in colonies, or groups. Living with other bats helps them keep warm. Bats **roost** high up to protect themselves from **predators**.

Some bats **hibernate** during the winter, when there is less food available. These bats find a cave and sleep for five or six months. They wake up in the spring when food can be found more easily.

To sleep, bats hang upside down so they can fly away quickly if needed.

Some bats migrate during the winter. These bats fly to warmer places when there is little food available in colder areas.

Bat Features

Many bats are known for flying through the night sky and eating insects. They have many features that help them do these tasks. For example, bat bones are very thin and light. This makes it easier for bats to fly.

HEAD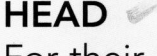
For their body size, bats have larger brains than birds. They are very smart. Bats can remember places and people for a long time.

WINGS
Bat wings are made of skin. Bats have long finger bones that support their wings. The wings stretch from the hind leg to the fingers. Bats have a thumb that is free from the wing. They use their thumb to cling to trees and ceilings. The largest bats in the world have wingspans of up to 6 feet (2 meters).

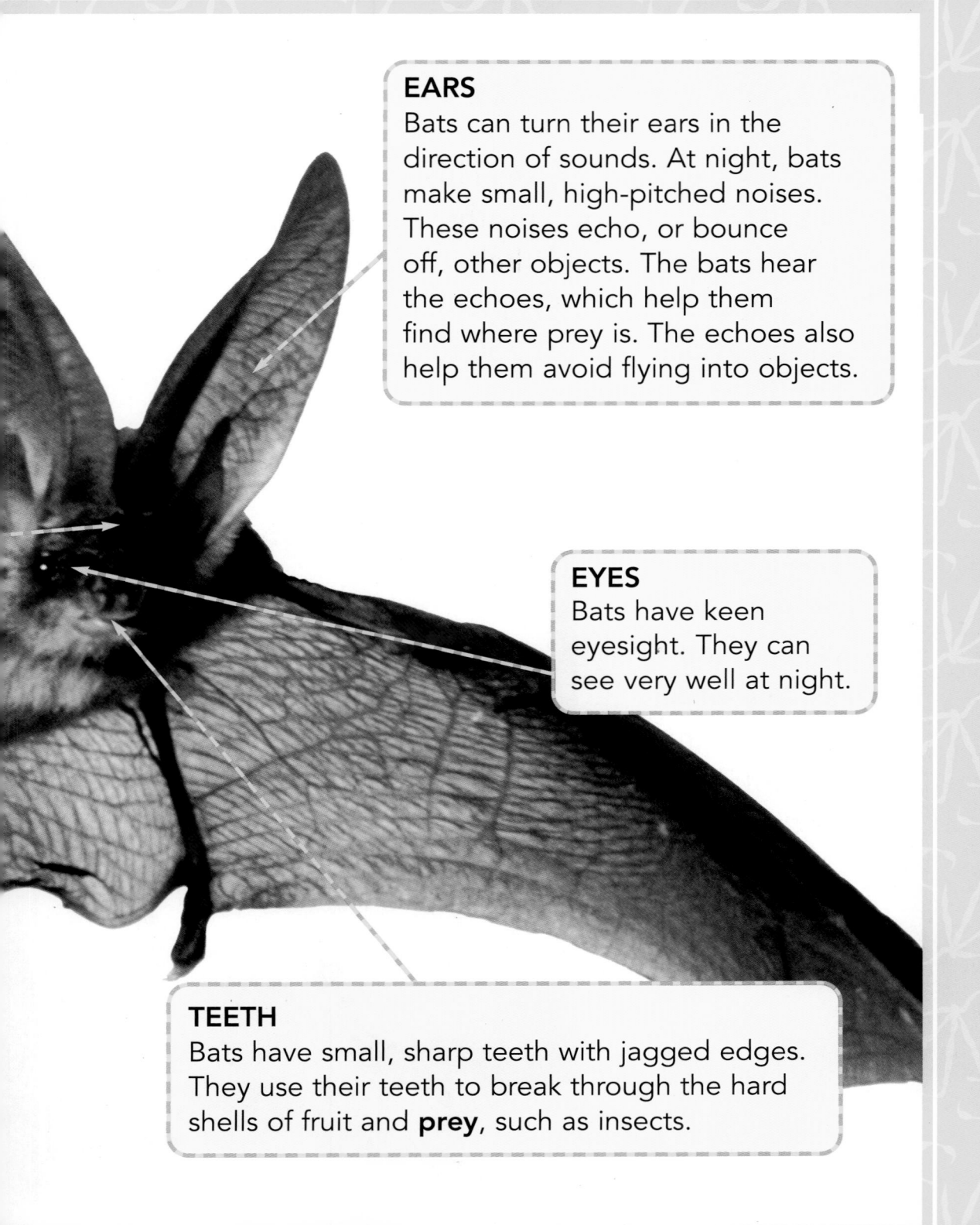

EARS

Bats can turn their ears in the direction of sounds. At night, bats make small, high-pitched noises. These noises echo, or bounce off, other objects. The bats hear the echoes, which help them find where prey is. The echoes also help them avoid flying into objects.

EYES

Bats have keen eyesight. They can see very well at night.

TEETH

Bats have small, sharp teeth with jagged edges. They use their teeth to break through the hard shells of fruit and **prey**, such as insects.

What Do Bats Eat?

Most bats are insectivores. This means they eat mostly insects, such as beetles, moths, mosquitoes, mayflies, and flying ants. Bats are helpful to humans because they eat insects that can spread disease and eat crops. A colony of bats can eat 250 tons (227,000 kg) of insects in one night.

Some bats are carnivores. This means they eat meat, such as small fish, reptiles, birds, and other mammals. Vampire bats drink blood from their prey.

Certain kinds of bats eat only fruit and nectar.

A bat can eat as much as half its own body weight in insects each night.

Bat Life Cycle

Bats mate before they hibernate. This happens in autumn or winter. Male bats sing a special song to attract female bats. Sometimes, one male bat will mate with more than 30 female bats.

Pups

At birth, most pups are blind, have no fur, and cannot fly. After a few days, their eyes open. Mother bats recognize their pups through scent and sound. Pups drink milk from their mother. They stay in the roost when their mother leaves to hunt.

Young Bats

Young bats grow very quickly. They can learn to fly and hunt in two to four weeks. Often, young bats cling to their mother when she roosts and flies.

Female bats give birth to one or two pups in a litter. Groups of female bats will roost together. Male bats roost apart from females.

Adult Bats

Bats live longer than other small animals. They can live for 10 to 20 years. The oldest known bat lived for more than 30 years.

Encountering Bats

Bats often live near people. Sometimes, they roost in attics and sheds. Special bat houses can be made from wood. Hanging a bat house outdoors in trees can keep bats from living inside buildings.

In rare cases, bats can carry **rabies**. It is important not to come into contact with bats. Family pets should be **vaccinated** against rabies in case they come into contact with a bat or another animal carrying the virus.

If you find an injured bat, do not approach it. It is best to call a wildlife officer. During the day, you may come across bats roosting. Try not to disturb them with noise or light.

Useful Websites

To learn more about bats, visit
**www.sandiegozoo.org/animalbytes/
t-bat.html**.

There are 45 bat species in the United States.

Myths and Legends

Many cultures have myths and legends about bats. Some people believe that bats are dangerous. Bats are sometimes shown as villains in movies and cartoons. Scary stories have been written about these winged animals. In some cases, people believed that bats were vampires or witches' companions.

In China, bats are symbols of happiness and good luck. Images of bats appear on Chinese jewelry, furniture, and **tapestries**. Chinese emperors had images of bats on their thrones and robes.

Batman is a comic book superhero who dresses like a bat.

A Bat Legend

This Ojibwa Indian Legend is about how the first bat was created.

One morning when Father Sun was rising, he got caught in some tree branches. When Father Sun did not appear the next day, the animals searched the forest. A squirrel was running through the treetops when he spotted Father Sun.

The squirrel ran toward Father Sun, but the heat burned off his tail, made his fur black, and nearly blinded him. The squirrel tried again to help Father Sun. He pushed hard until Father Sun was free. Father Sun felt bad that the little squirrel was burned while helping him.

"What do you want more than anything in the world?" Father Sun asked the squirrel. The squirrel replied, "I have always wanted to fly."

Father Sun granted the squirrel's wish. The little squirrel became the first bat.

Frequently Asked Questions

When is the best time of day to see bats in nature?

Answer: The best time to see bats is at dusk, when they are leaving their roosts to hunt. Bats can often be seen flying around lights at night. The lights attract insects, and the bats will hunt for insects around lights.

Do bats have predators?

Answer: Bats have many predators, including snakes, hawks, weasels, owls, cats, dogs, and humans. In Venezuela, there is a large **centipede** that hunts bats.

Do bats live in caves?

Answer: Bats often live in caves. Sometimes, thousands or millions of bats will roost together in a cave. Caves offer a safe shelter for bats as they sleep. Few predators can reach them as they hang from the top of a cave.

Puzzler

See if you can answer these questions about bats.

1. What are the two main kinds of bats?
2. What are a bat's wings made out of?
3. How many pups are in a litter of bats?
4. How long do bats live in nature?
5. What do bats eat?

Answers: 1. megabats and microbats 2. finger bones covered by thin layers of skin 3. one or two 4. 10 to 20 years 5. blood, nectar, insects, fish, and other animals

Find Out More

There are many more interesting facts to learn about bats. Look for these and other books at your library.

Mason, Adrienne. *Bats*. Kids Can Press, 2003.

Swanson, Diane. *Welcome to the World of Bats*. Whitecap Books, 1998.

Words to Know

centipede: a wormlike animal

fossil: ancient remains of an animal or plant

grooming: cleaning the fur or skin

hibernate: to spend the winter in an inactive state

mammals: animals that have fur, make milk, and are born live

nectar: sugary fluid that comes from plants

predators: animals that hunt other animals for food

prey: an animal that is hunted or caught for food

rabies: a disease caused by a virus that can be passed from animals to other animals and humans

roost: a place where animals sleep

saliva: a watery fluid created in the mouth

species: groups of animals or plants that have many features in common

strokes: blockages or bleeding from a blood vessel leading to the brain

tapestries: thick woven fabrics with designs on them

tropical: hot and humid climate

vaccinated: being protected from a disease

Index

24